Pilot Testing a Pika Monitoring Protocol in Glacier National Park

Project Report 2012

Natural Resource Technical Report NPS/UCBN/NRTR—2013/667

Mackenzie Jeffress[1], Jami Belt[2], Tara Carolin[2], Thomas J. Rodhouse[3], and Mike Britten[4]

[1]National Park Service
Upper Columbia Basin Network
105 E. 2nd St., Suite 5
Moscow, ID 83843

[2]National Park Service
Glacier National Park
Crown of the Continent Research Learning Center
P.O. Box 128
West Glacier, MT 59936

[3]National Park Service
Upper Columbia Basin Network
63095 Deschutes Market Road
Bend, OR 97701

[4]National Park Service
Rocky Mountain Network
Natural Resources Program Center
1201 Oakridge Drive, Suite 200
Fort Collins, CO 80525

January 2013

U.S. Department of the Interior
National Park Service
Natural Resource Stewardship and Science
Fort Collins, Colorado

The National Park Service, Natural Resource Stewardship and Science office in Fort Collins, Colorado, publishes a range of reports that address natural resource topics. These reports are of interest and applicability to a broad audience in the National Park Service and others in natural resource management, including scientists, conservation and environmental constituencies, and the public.

The Natural Resource Technical Report Series is used to disseminate results of scientific studies in the physical, biological, and social sciences for both the advancement of science and the achievement of the National Park Service mission. The series provides contributors with a forum for displaying comprehensive data that are often deleted from journals because of page limitations.

All manuscripts in the series receive the appropriate level of peer review to ensure that the information is scientifically credible, technically accurate, appropriately written for the intended audience, and designed and published in a professional manner. This report received informal peer review by subject-matter experts who were not directly involved in the collection, analysis, or reporting of the data.

Views, statements, findings, conclusions, recommendations, and data in this report do not necessarily reflect views and policies of the National Park Service, U.S. Department of the Interior. Mention of trade names or commercial products does not constitute endorsement or recommendation for use by the U.S. Government.

This report is available from (http://science.nature.nps.gov/im/units/ucbn/) and the Natural Resource Publications Management website (http://www.nature.nps.gov/publications/nrpm/).

Please cite this publication as:

NPS 117/119606, January 2013

Contents

Figures

Tables

Appendices

Abstract

The American pika (*Ochotona princeps*) is considered an indicator species for detecting ecological effects of climate change. Understanding pika population trends over time can provide important insights to park managers about potential impacts of climate change on park ecosystems. Pika monitoring is underway in several national park units across the western U.S. and this report describes the pilot effort to implement a standardized pika monitoring protocol in Glacier National Park, Montana. From July through September 2012, 47 pika monitoring sites were established and surveyed for pika site occupancy in the park. Sites were established along trails (up to 10 km from the trailhead) and within 100 m from trails, and occupancy of sites was determined by searching for pikas, pika calls, fresh haypiles, and fresh scat within 12-m radius plots. The proportion of sites surveyed that were considered occupied based on these detections was high at 0.81. Pikas were detected across the range of elevation of sites surveyed and throughout the areas surveyed in the park. Given the active citizen science program being coordinated by the park's Crown of the Continent Research Learning Center and the interest in having citizen scientists conduct the pika monitoring long term, citizen scientists were trained and conducted resurveys of the established sites. This provided an opportunity to compare the detection results between field technicians and citizen scientists and to identify ways to make pika monitoring feasible for implementation by citizen scientists in the future. A customized relational database application, implemented in Microsoft Access, was used to store and manipulate the data associated with this project and all project-related files have been provided to the park. Since this was funded as a 1-year pilot effort, the monitoring goals and responsibilities will be turned over to the park staff in 2013.

Acknowledgments

Funding for this project was provided by the National Park Service Climate Change Response Program. L. Garrett, G. Dicus, M. Biel, and P. Wilson provided valuable insights in the planning process of this pilot effort. M. Lonneker coordinated GIS analyses and data management, including creating and managing the Access database. M. Ratchford and K. Kranzler, University of Idaho field technicians, worked long, hard days to establish survey sites and coordinated many aspects of the field efforts, and two citizen science technicians, J. Porter and A. Strom, trained the citizen scientists and helped with many of the logistical tasks. We are also grateful for the 12 citizen scientists who volunteered their time conducting resurveys of the pika sites.

Introduction

The American pika (*Ochotona princeps*) is a small mammal related to rabbits and hares that inhabits rocky, often montane environments of western North America from British Columbia south to northern New Mexico (Hall 1981). Concerns regarding the pika's vulnerability to global climate change are growing, and many are considering the pika as a climate change indicator species (Smith 1974, McDonald and Brown 1992, Lawlor 1998, Beever et al. 2003, 2010, 2011, Krajick 2004, Smith et al. 2004, Grayson 2005). In some areas of the Great Basin localized extirpations of pika populations have been documented (Beever et al. 2003, Grayson 2005, Beever et al. 2010) and the species' range appears to have contracted as a response to climate change during the Holocene and last century (Hafner 1994, Hafner and Sullivan 1995, Beever et al. 2003, Grayson 2005, Moritz et al. 2008, Galbreath et al. 2009). The hypothesized mechanism for these range contractions is elevated temperatures and decreased mountain snowpack resulting from accelerated climate change (Smith et al. 2004, Grayson 2005). Although in 2010 listing of the American pika under the Endangered Species Act was deemed not warranted, the US Fish and Wildlife Service recognized that "climate change is a potential threat to the long-term survival of the American pika" and the agency called for further data on the status, trends, and determinants of pika distribution for future listing and management considerations (Crist 2010). The National Park Service's initiation of pika monitoring in several parks is an attempt to address these information gaps.

Pikas are popular and charismatic animals at Glacier National Park. A recent (2007-2009) survey of pikas and their habitat in the park conducted by Moyer-Horner (2011) identified 400 suitable habitat patches and documented a relatively large pika population (2071-4052 individuals) within the park. The park also has a very active citizen science program coordinated by the Crown of the Continent Research Learning Center with volunteers collecting scientific data on pikas, mountain goats, loons, aquatic macroinvertebrates, and others. This program led Moyer-Horner et al. (2012) to examine the ability of participants, including field technicians and citizen scientists, with wide ranges of experience and training to collect reliable data. Although Moyer-Horner et al. (2012) found that citizen scientists can collect reliable data via sitting surveys (focusing on visual and aural detections), they found that citizen scientists could not adequately estimate pika densities. However, this type of observer comparison has not occurred with the site occupancy survey methodologies described in the Jeffress et al. (2011) pika monitoring protocol that is being used widely in the National Park Service.

The purpose of this project was to pilot test a peer-reviewed, long-term pika monitoring protocol (Jeffress et al. 2011) for the American pika (*Ochotona princeps*) in Glacier National Park. The pika is a climate-sensitive species and this effort provided new information on the distribution, survey methodologies, and habitat associations of the species in the park. In particular, this project established long-term monitoring sites to estimate the proportion of sample sites occupied by pikas and assessed detectability of pika using both direct and indirect evidence of pika presence (via visuals, aurals, scat, and haypiles) for observers with various levels of experience and training. We worked with the Crown of the Continent Research Learning Center Citizen Science Program to evaluate the feasibility and effectiveness of citizen scientists in protocol implementation. Surveys were conducted summer 2012 and beginning in 2013, the park will take control of the monitoring of these sites, if funding is available.

Methods

Using a modified version of the Jeffress et al. (2011) protocol, we initiated this effort by identifying potential pika habitat and defining a sampling design for selecting monitoring sites. We then trained observers to conduct surveys in 12-m radius circular plots using standardized survey methods and data forms. Citizen scientists resurveyed the sites and field technicians entered the data into a customized Access database. These steps are detailed in the following sections.

Site Selection

Using a combination of existing GIS shapefiles provided by the park (file "Merge_All_Talus_Potential_Habitat.shp" stored in the GLAC project file directory in the DVD provided to the park and available upon request from the UCBN), including a potential pika talus habitat map created by L. Moyer-Horner and the park vegetation map, we identified ~32 trails (files: "10k_trailsselected_20120511.shp" and "talus_100m_Roads_class1trails.shp") and several road sites that had potential pika habitat of slopes < 35° and within 100 m of the trail or road. These areas were targeted for field sampling.

Each surveying effort began with the field technicians conducting an exploratory hike out 10 km or to the end of the trail, whichever came first. GPS coordinates for guidance as to where the trail starts, ends, and intersects other trails were provided. Also, coordinates for the center of mapped potential habitat patches that met our sampling criteria were provided to the technicians; however, it is important to note that patches on the maps often did not represent what was actually on the ground. Sometimes mapped habitat was not present on the ground and sometimes potential habitat was encountered but not identified using the GIS shapefiles. Therefore, technicians marked (with a GPS) the start and ending coordinates for each talus patch encountered (whether it was currently identified in the potential habitat map or not) along or near the trail (i.e., line-of-sight and within 100 m) and noted the approximate size of each patch (i.e., roughly < 1 football field = small patch; > 1 football field = large patch; Appendix A and Figure 1).

At the end of each trail, the technicians counted the number of talus patches encountered and based on the patch size, how many sites could be placed in each patch. If the patch was generally less than or equal to one football field in size (average area of 4,460 m^2), one site could be placed in that patch; if greater than one football field in size, two sites could be placed in that patch. The number of sites per trail was dependent on the length and habitat abundance and sites had to be a minimum of 50 m apart.

After the exploratory hike and as the technicians were hiking back toward the trailhead, they attempted to establish and survey as many of the sites identified for that trail as time allowed that day. However, some trails required multiple days to survey. Once the technicians encounter the first talus edge, they hiked 25 m father along the trail and stopped and evaluated the habitat. Distances were measured using a GPS unit and/or rangefinder. If the talus slope was accessible within 100 m in both left and right directions (perpendicular from the trail) they flipped a coin to determine which direction to go. Once direction was established the technician used a random distance chart to determine where to place the first site. The chart provided a list of randomized distances (12-100 m; 12 m minimum from the trail so the plot would not overlap with the trail).

At that point, the technicians began to establish a site for surveying and recorded the distance and direction used on the data form. If for some reason the technicians were not able to establish a site from 25 m along the trail (e.g., due to irregularly shaped talus, etc.), they walked another 5 m along the trail and evaluated if a site could be placed from there. The 5 m increments continued until a site could be established. The reverse was also possible for very small patches (i.e., 20 m or 15 m along the trail).

If a second site was to be established (= large patch), the technicians returned to the trail from the first site and hiked another 50 m along the trail (or halfway to the far end of the patch if it was a large patch, whichever was the farthest distance) to establish the second site. Once this distance was met, the technicians used the same criteria (i.e., new random distance, coin flip, etc.) as the first site. Please see Figure 1 for a hypothetical example of site establishment along a trail.

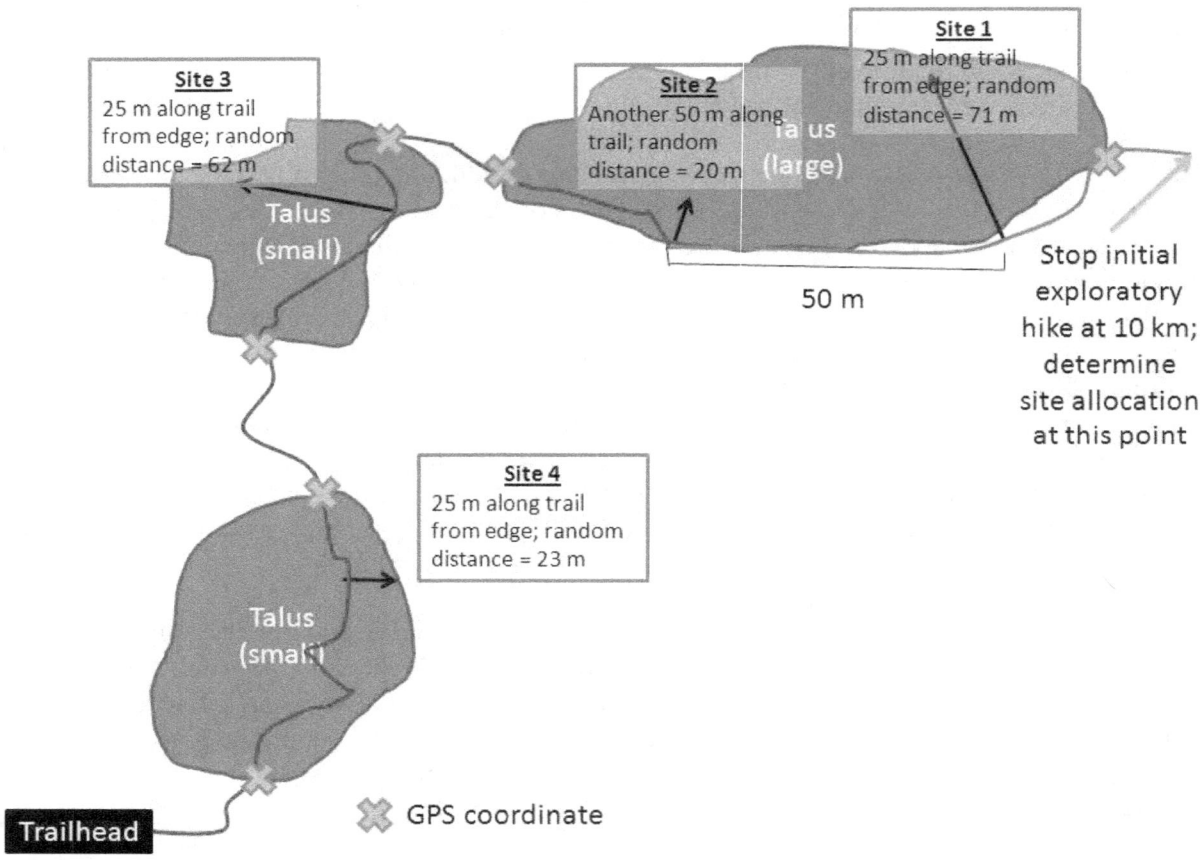

Figure 1. Example of site establishment. Please note that this diagram is not to scale.

All sites met the required potential habitat definition (see Table 1). Safety and ease of access was considered when establishing sites. As stated below, sites were not placed on slopes >35° or slopes that were perceived to be dangerous or unstable. The same considerations were made for the route to access the site; keeping in mind that citizen scientists/volunteers of varying skill/ability levels for hiking and/or cross-country navigation using a GPS unit would be resurveying the sites. A field manual describing these site selection and survey procedures was

4

provided to the field technicians for reference
(PikaMonitoringManual_GLAC_Techs_20120713.docx).

Table 1. Criteria used for establishing a pika monitoring site in 2012.

Criteria for a site
The site must contain ≥10% target habitat. Target habitat includes talus, lava, outcrops or other forms of creviced rock that can provide shelter for pikas. Please note that scree or collections of small rocks (< 6 inches across) do not provide sufficient shelter for pikas.
The site must not be dangerous/prohibitively difficult to work on (e.g., slope >35°, rockfall imminent, or other unsafe conditions).
The site should be relatively snow-free (<10% snow cover). If the site has not yet experienced snowmelt (e.g., site is being surveyed early July), the site should be surveyed at a later date.
The site should be a minimum of 50 m for any other site as well as at least 12 m from the trail (so the search area does not overlap the trail), and no more than 100 m from the trail.

Occupancy Surveys

A site was defined as a 12-m radius plot containing ≥10% target habitat (see definition of target habitat in Table 1). Once the technician(s) reached the location for a site center (see "Site Selection"), the center was marked with an aluminum tree tag and rock cairn. The 12-m radius search area was temporary marked using a pre-measured cord and orange pin flags. One surveyor then thoroughly searched the entire plot and recorded all evidence of pika activity that he/she detected, including pika sightings, calls, scat, and hay. Information about the detection(s), including time, distance to center, number of scat pellets (if applicable), was also recorded. Once the surveyor felt the survey was complete (with a minimum search time of 15 minutes and suggested maximum of 30 minutes), the end time was noted. The technician(s) then conducted a vegetation survey, estimating the percentage of the plot that was rock, bare, graminoid (i.e., grasses), forbs (i.e., flowering, non-woody plants), shrubs, and trees (Appendix B). Finally, the technician(s) recorded directions and took photos of the site and the route to access the site in order to develop site location maps for the citizen scientists.

Citizen Science Resurveys

The Citizen Science Program of the Crown of the Continent Research Learning Center coordinated the citizen scientists' resurveys of sites. The technicians provided site guides to the Citizen Science Program coordinator who was responsible for training technicians and assigned scientists to survey sites. The technicians also produced a training video (available on YouTube: http://youtu.be/cP8iUfM2XpE) and an example completed data form to further help the citizen scientists understand the survey procedures. The citizen scientists were provided with field kits, which included pre-loaded GPS units, surveying equipment, etc. Citizen scientist data forms were a modified version of the original data forms and included a brief questionnaire about the surveying experience (Appendix C). Once surveys were completed, the citizen scientists provided the hard copy data forms back to the Citizen Science Program coordinator who then provided copies to the technicians for data entry.

Results

Site Selection

From July to September 2012, 20 trail segments (up to 10 km along the trail) and three potential roads sites were explored for potential pika habitat and pika sites by the field technicians. A description of trails surveyed and talus patches encountered is provided in GLAC_TrailAndTalusInfo_20120920.xls. With only several exceptions, including one avalanche forest knockdown along the Lake Josephine/North Piegan Pass Trail where a field of downed trees was identified as potential habitat, most of the potential habitat identified was rock, the majority of which was talus. However, only two of the potential roadside sites identified were suitable for survey sites, of which a site just east of Avalanche Creek was established. A roadside site in Many Glacier would be suitable talus; however, the area was inaccessible due to protection for habitat restoration. After establishing sites, the technicians developed and frequently updated a spreadsheet titled "High Country Citizen Science Pika Sites" (Pika_Site_List_sitesmapped_20120917.xlsx) to help citizen scientists identify the sites they wished to survey.

Occupancy Surveys

The technicians established and surveyed 47 sites (GLAC_2012_Occupancy.shp). Elevation of sites ranged from 1049 – 2301 m (3441 – 7549 ft) with a mean elevation of 1906 m (6255 ft). Based on the surveys conducted by the hired field technicians, 38 sites were considered occupied, one site had only old sign, and nine sites lacked any evidence of pika activity within the plot. Therefore, 81% of sites surveyed were considered occupied based on the field technician surveys (Figure 4). Mean elevation of occupied sites was 1913 m and mean elevation of unoccupied sites was 1878 m. Since previous studies in other areas have found that occupied sites tend to have more forbs and less grasses than unoccupied sites (Rodhouse et al. 2010; Jeffress et al. *in press*), we chose to examine this for our 2012 sites in Glacier. No clear trend presented itself in this analysis (Figures 2 and 3).

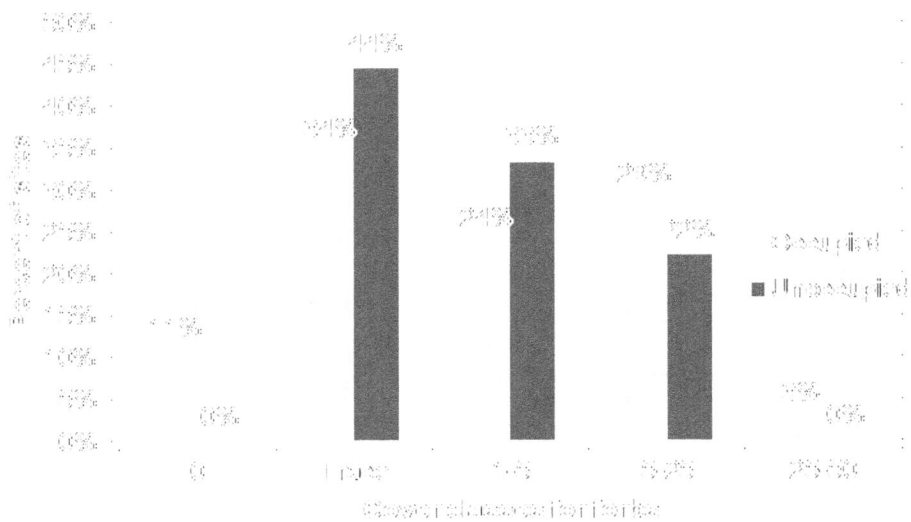

Figure 2. A comparison of forb cover estimates for occupied and unoccupied sites.

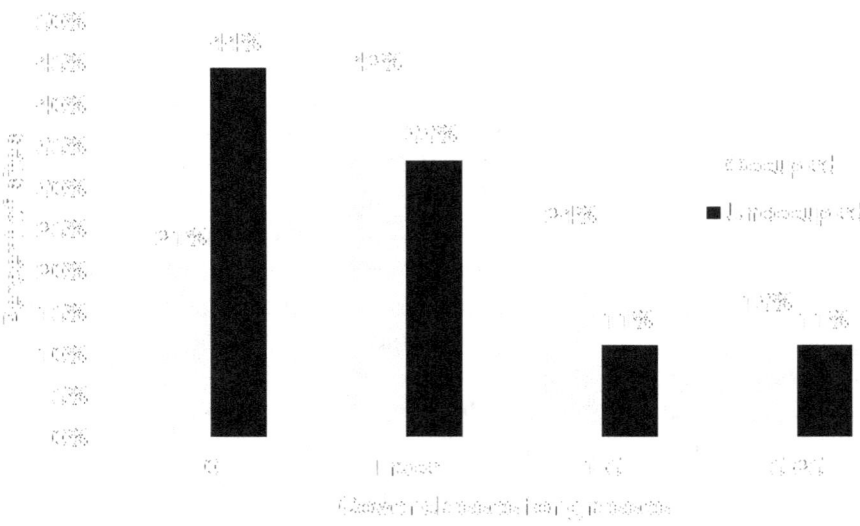

Figure 3. A comparison of graminoid (grasses) cover estimate for occupied and unoccupied sites.

Citizen science resurveys

A total of 25 resurveys of 19 sites established and initially surveyed by the field technicians were resurveyed by 12 citizen scientists. Two additional surveys were attempted but the citizen scientist did not feel comfortable accessing the sites. We note that the number of sites resurveyed by citizen scientists in 2012 was limited due to the fact that many sites were not established until later in the summer. For example, only 21 sites had been established and mapped by the time of the goat/pika blitz organized by the citizen science program, which occurred the third weekend of August. Now that sites have already been established and mapped, it is likely that citizen scientists will be able to conduct more resurveys in future years.

A comparison of the initial/technician survey results to the citizen scientist resurveys showed a significant difference in detectability. Only 32% (8) of the citizen scientist resurveys agreed with the initial survey results. In all cases where the citizen scientist resurvey results differed from the initial technician survey results, the technician survey found the site to be occupied and the citizen scientist resurveys found either only old sign or no pika evidence within the plot. Also, one of the concerns was the ability of citizen scientists to collect information on vegetation cover. We therefore compared the cover estimates of the technicians, with more experience at estimating vegetation cover, to the citizen science data and found that more than half of the estimates (52%) were consistent. Furthermore, when there were discrepancies between the estimates, there typically (35% of estimates) was only a difference of one cover class (e.g., "Trace" versus "1-5%"). Only 13% of the estimates by citizen scientists were greater than one cover classes different from the technician estimates.

Citizen scientist questionnaire on data form

We were able to use the questionnaire responses from 28 of the citizen science resurvey data forms. The scientists ranked the ability to traverse talus, the ability to navigate to/locate the site marker and the ability to age pika haypiles and scat as the most difficult tasks for pika surveys (Table 1); however, even these were ranked from easy to somewhat difficult. All other tasks

8

were ranked from very easy to easy. Average reported time to locate the marker was 8.3 minutes (11 responses). The most common reason for the citizen scientist to select that site was that it was a scenic area (13), followed by optimal hiking (8), and the site being in a new area (6). Other reasons less reported were optimal driving (2), safety considerations (2), and that the site was along a planned trip/trail (write-in; 10). The average reported number of sites completed by citizen scientists in a day was two. One citizen scientist reported that he did not feel comfortable accessing two sites (038 and 039). We also noted that the ranking of some of these variables, such as the ability to reach and traverse talus slopes, changes significantly depending on the site.

Table 2. Ratings for citizen science questionnaire regarding the ability to complete various survey tasks.

Please rate the following for this site on a scale of 1-5 (1 = very easy; 5 = very difficult)	Number of respondents	Ranking
Ability to reach the talus field	26	Very easy – easy (1.7)
Ability to traverse talus	27	Somewhat difficult (2.9)
Ability to navigate to/locate the site marker	25	Easy – somewhat difficult (2.5)
Ability to follow/understand the instructions and survey methods	25	Easy (1.8)
Ability to identify pikas	10	Very easy – easy (1.4)
Ability to identify pika sign	18	Very easy – easy (1.4)
Ability to age pika haypiles and scat	13	Easy – somewhat difficult (2.3)
Ability to complete search in allotted time	20	Easy (1.9)
Ability to estimate vegetation cover	20	Easy (2.1)

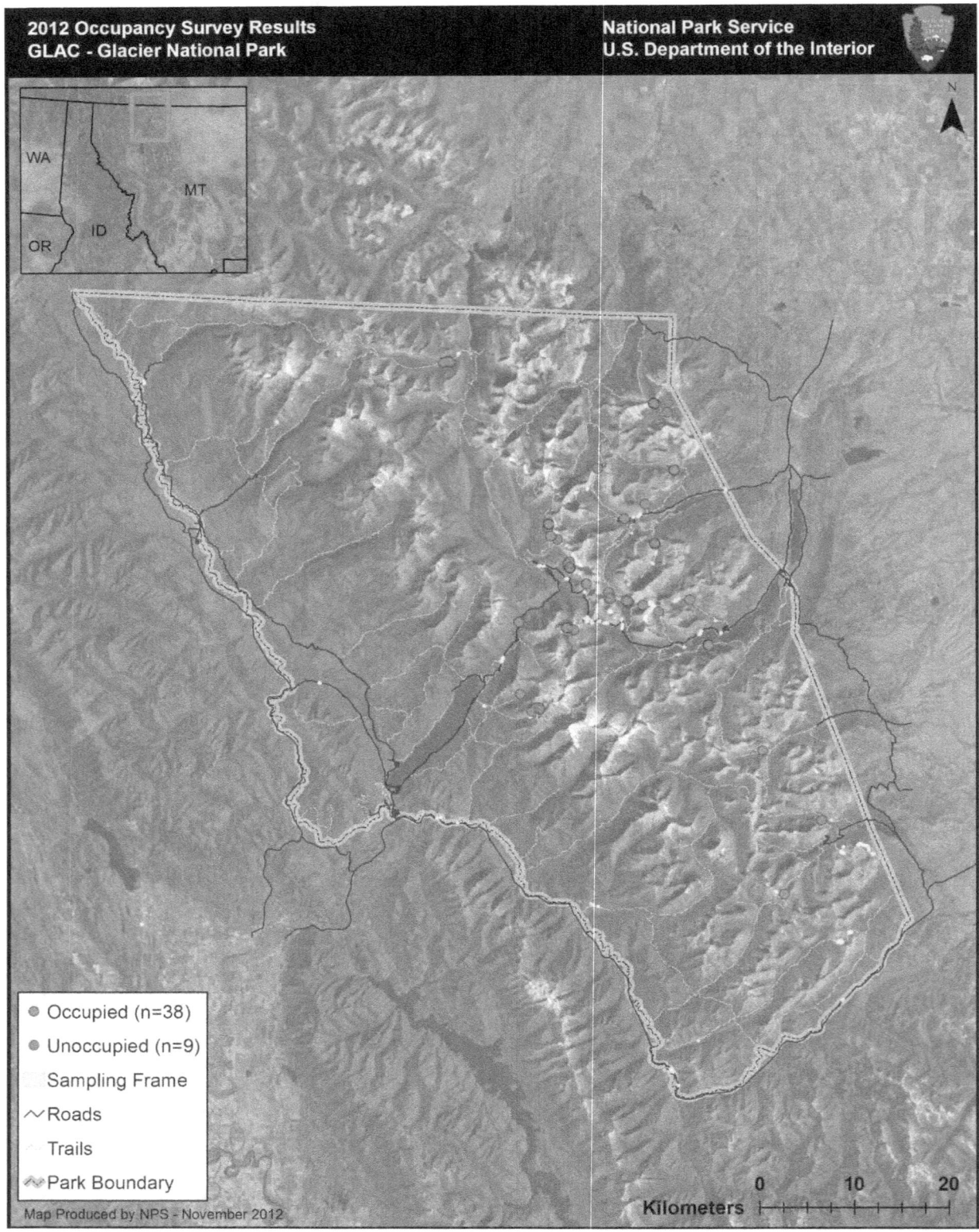

Figure 4. Map of sites established and survey results for 2012.

Discussion

The 2012 pika monitoring pilot effort was considered a success on many levels. All trails and road sites initially identified for surveys were explored and 47 sites established. Site occupancy was high (81%) suggesting that pikas currently occupied a vast majority of the potential habitat at the park. We saw no evidence of a lower elevational limit for pikas, although this could change in the future and a more thorough analysis of pika distribution along the elevational gradient should be conducted in GLAC. Furthermore, we saw no significant influence of forb or graminoid cover, which other studies, particularly those on the edge of the species' distribution and often in drier climates, have seen (e.g., Rodhouse et al. 2010). This is possibly because Glacier National Park is on the interior of the species' range and may be a "safer" core area for pikas. However, with predicted climate change these relationships may change in the future, reinforcing the need to monitor these sites and use any information regarding site losses as an early warning indicator.

Several issues presented themselves throughout this project and here we take an opportunity to provide suggestions for improving the monitoring design for future implementation in the park. First, in the planning efforts for not only Glacier National Park but other parks as well, accurately mapping potential habitat has proven challenging. We found that using the combination of maps previously developed for the park was the best indicator of areas to search but opportunities to improve these maps should be pursued, especially if any predictive mapping efforts are desired (see Rodhouse et al. 2010 for example). Furthermore, the field technicians and citizen scientists often noted that more potential habitat was available but did not fall within the strict 100 m buffer. Particularly, the technicians felt this cutoff impacted their ability to establish a large number of sites. They noted that they frequently encountered potential habitat within 100-500 m from the trail and many of the areas would have been fairly easy to access. If the park desires more sites for long-term monitoring, the buffer could be extended to capture more of this potential habitat. If this approach is chosen, we suggest using trained technicians or field personnel to properly identify these sites and use discretion regarding safety (erring on the side of caution).

In their end of the season reports (KKranzler_EndofSeasonReport_20120920.doc and MRatchford_EndofSeasonReport_20120926.docx), the field technicians also noted that the suggested 30 minute maximum search time was sometimes too short, particularly for structurally complex sites or sites with a large amount of sign. One technician noted that sometimes the search took up to 1 hour, even with someone else recording data. Similar concerns were expressed by the citizen scientists and this may help explain some of the false absences (described below). Since the point of monitoring is to maximize detectability for the best estimate of occupancy, we suggest extending the suggested maximum search time to 1 hour. This should be done while noting that the search period recommendations are to prevent surveyors from spending several hours until they find something or searching the same area over and over, thus biasing search effort. Another option to consider for long-term monitoring is to end the search once a fresh detection (i.e., visual, aural, fresh hay, or fresh scat) has been made within the plot. Although this has not yet been done in the other parks using the Jeffress et al. (2011) protocol, it would allow for a "time-saving" survey effort that still captures the primary occupancy information.

Another issue encountered was with the data forms completed by the citizen scientists. Technicians had a hard time entering citizen science data due to blank spaces or information not recorded properly on the data form, including site numbers. Consequently, opportunities to improve the citizen science data form presented themselves during data entry. The problems encountered and suggestions for improvement are as follows:

- **Site numbers were not always recorded**: Have the citizen scientists record site UTMs along with the site number. Then, if they don't record the site number, the UTMs could be used to determine which site they surveyed.

- **Missing or incomplete fields on data form:** These were most often for vegetation cover but also for sign type and others. Wherever there is an opportunity, provide a list of the options for that field (e.g., "0", "T", … for cover) and ask the citizen scientists to circle just one. This could also be done for detection type. Also, the fact that no field should be left blank could be emphasized during training (e.g., suggest writing "NA").

- **Time not recorded as military time:** Either make it clear that military time is desired (e.g., say "2400") or provide an AM / PM option to circle.

Improving the data forms and placing more emphasis on the concepts behind the survey methodologies, such as focusing on detections within the plot instead of outside of the plot, and data recording (i.e., complete data forms) during training may also help with some of these issues. However, we recognize that the citizen science program is constantly working on these types of training improvements and incomplete data forms are likely a struggle for many citizen science survey efforts.

Moyer-Horner et al. (2012) found that citizen scientists collected comparable data to that of technicians for visual and aural pika surveys but that technicians were better at detecting sign than volunteers. Our results are similar, where citizen scientists are missing a substantial amount of pika evidence found previously by the technicians, particularly fresh hay and fresh scat. These types of differences are referred to as "false absences" and can partially be accounted for with multiple resurveys to estimate detection probability. It is likely that the false absences / low detectability during resurveys by citizen scientists is due to their lack of confidence in identifying pika sign and/or their inexperience with these types of surveys. Anecdotally, it also appears the citizen scientists focused more on detections, particularly pika vocalizations and visuals, outside of the plot, especially at sites where the search area was in less than "ideal" pika habitat and "ideal" pika habitat was nearby. Some citizen scientists even noted that the plot should be moved to a nearby area where they saw or heard pikas. Since recording detections outside of the plot was an option to help note activity in the area and not essential to the monitoring, this option could be removed to focus citizen scientists on detections within the survey plot. Also, many of these issues, such as improving citizen scientist confidence in identifying and aging sign, could be emphasized during future trainings. We've found with other crews that "in the field" training is the best to help surveyors develop the "search image" for pikas and pika sign. Similarly, some citizen scientists noted that they were only able to complete one or two surveys and they needed more practice to be more comfortable with the new methodologies. Furthermore, the training site, which was chosen for accessibility, did not have fresh pika sign for the citizen scientists to observe so in the future we recommend, when possible, collecting fresh scat to use during training and/or looking for better training sites with more pika activity. Although we ultimately recognize that citizen scientists appear to be more comfortable identifying pikas by sight and call, we do not recommend removing the sign search from the survey procedures as this would likely increase the occurrence of false absences and lead to an underestimation of occupancy.

Although, we cannot completely rule out that a seasonal effect could also be affecting the resurveys, other studies and pika surveying efforts have found high detectability when using technicians with a wildlife education background and typically detectability has improved as the season progresses (not declined as we saw here). A positive aspect of these results is that they do not suggest the occurrence of false positives (i.e., misidentify sign or saying an animal is present when it is not), which would be harder to account for, for the citizen scientist resurveys. Given these results, we encourage the continued documentation of detections with vouchers (i.e., photos or samples collected) when possible. Furthermore, if citizen scientists are used to implement monitoring in the future, multiple resurveys at each site should be conducted to provide multiple opportunities to detect if a site is occupied.

The results from the citizen science questionnaire could also be used to strengthen planning and training efforts in the future. For example, given the difficulty for some citizen scientists to access the sites, additional training on GPS use and identifying site markers may prove helpful. Similarly, one citizen scientist noted that two sites were too difficult to access. In this case, a difficulty ranking/measure for each site might help citizen scientists determine which sites are appropriate for them based on their capabilities and comfort levels. For example, some citizen scientists are backpacking for the surveys and they could use this information to determine that the site is too steep or difficult to access with heavy overnight packs. However, in summary the citizen scientists collected useful data, including cover estimates that were comparable to the technicians' estimates. Furthermore, the citizen scientists appeared to enjoy the pika surveys and we suggest this type of effort continue to be utilized.

All data files produced as a result of this effort are being provided to the park on a DVD and will also be kept on file with the UCBN. There is no long-term funding for this project; however, the hope is that in 2013 the park resources staff and Crown of the Continent Research Learning Center Citizen Science Program can use the results of this effort to resurvey/monitor the established sites. If additional sites are desired, we suggest allowing sites to reach further into the backcountry along trails and/or increasing the allowable distance from trails for sites.

Literature Cited

Beever, E. A., C. Ray, P. W. Mote, and J. L. Wilkening. 2010. Testing alternative models of climate-mediated extirpation. Ecological Applications 20:164-178.

Beever, E. A., C. Ray, J. L. Wilkening, P. W. Mote, and P. F. Brussard. 2011. Contemporary climate change alters the pace and drivers of extinction. Global Change Biology 17(6):1–17.

Beever, E. A., P. E. Brussard, and J. Berger. 2003. Patterns of apparent extirpation among isolated populations of pikas (*Ochotona princeps*) in the Great Basin. Journal of Mammalogy 84:37-54.

Crist, L. 2010. Endangered and threatened wildlife and plants; 12-month finding on a petition to list the American pika as threatened or endangered. FWS-R6-ES-2009-0021. U.S. Fish and Wildlife Service, Utah Ecological Services Field Office, West Valley City, Utah.

Galbreath, K. E., D. J. Hafner, and K. Zamudio. 2009. When cold is better: climate-driven elevation shifts yield complex patterns of diversification and demography in an alpine specialist (American pika, *Ochotona princeps*). Evolution 63:2848-2863.

Grayson, D. K. 2005. A brief history of Great Basin pikas. Journal of Biogeography 32:2103-2111.

Hafner, D. J. 1994. Pikas and permafrost: Post-Wisconsin zoogeography of *Ochotona* in the southern Rocky Mountains, USA. Arctic and Alpine Research 26:375–382.

Hafner, D. J., and R. M. Sullivan 1995. Historical and ecological biogeography of nearctic pikas (Lagomorpha: Ochotonidae). Journal of Mammalogy 76:302-321.

Hall, E. R. 1981. The mammals of North America. John Wiley & Sons, New York, NY.

Jeffress, M. R., J. Apel, L. K. Garrett, G. Holm, D. Larson, N. Nordensten, and T. J. Rodhouse. 2011. Monitoring the American pika (*Ochotona princeps*) in the Pacific West Region – Crater Lake National Park, Craters of the Moon National Monument and Preserve, Lassen Volcanic National Park, and Lava Beds National Monument: Narrative Version 1.0. Natural Resource Report NPS/UCBN/NRR-2011/336. National Park Service, Fort Collins, Colorado.

Jeffress, M. R., T. J. Rodhouse, C. Ray, S. Wolff, and C. Epps. *In review*. The idiosyncrasies of place: geographic variation in the climate-distribution relationship of the American pika. Ecological Applications.

Krajick, K. 2004. All downhill from here. Science 303:1600-1602.

Lawlor, T. E. 1998. Biogeography of Great Basin mammals: paradigm lost? Journal of Mammalogy 79:1111-1130.

McDonald, K. A., and J. J. Brown. 1992. Using montane mammals to model extinctions due to global change. Conservation Biology 6:409-415.

Moritz, C., J. L. Patton, C. J. Conroy, J. L. Parra, G. C. White, and S. R. Beissinger. 2008. Impact of a century of climate change on small-mammal communities in Yosemite National Park, USA. Science 322:261-264.

Moyer-Horner, L. 2011. American pika distribution, behavior, and observer variability. Dissertation, University of Wisconsin, Madison.

Moyer-Horner, L., M. M. Smith, and J. Belt. 2012. Citizen science and observer variability during American pika surveys. The Journal of Wildlife Management 76:1472-1479.

Rodhouse, T. J., E. A. Beever, L. K. Garrett, K. M. Irvine, M. R. Jeffress, M. Munts, and C. Ray. 2010. Distribution of American pikas in a low-elevation lava landscape: conservation implications from the range periphery. Journal of Mammalogy 91:1287-1299.

Smith, A. T. 1974. The distribution and dispersal of pikas: influences of behavior and climate. Ecology 55:1368-1376.

Smith, A. T., W. Li and D.S. Hik. 2004. Pikas as harbingers of global warming. Species 41:4-5.

Appendix A. Data Form 1 – Trails and Talus Information (Glacier 2012)

Date:

Observers:

Trail name:

Trails and talus information (Glacier 2012)

Patch	Start UTMX	Start UTMY	Distance from trail*	End UTMX	End UTMY	Distance from trail*	Patch size	Patch sketched on map?	Site ID #s (NA if no sites established in patch)	Comments
Patch 1							Large / small	Yes / No		
Patch 2							Large / small	Yes / No		
Patch 3							Large / small	Yes / No		
Patch 4							Large / small	Yes / No		
Patch 5							Large / small	Yes / No		
Patch 6							Large / small	Yes / No		
Patch 7							Large / small	Yes / No		
Patch 8							Large / small	Yes / No		
Patch 9							Large / small	Yes / No		
Patch 10							Large / small	Yes / No		

*Only record if the start/stop of the patch edge does not intersect the trail.

Appendix B. Data Form 2 – Initial Pika Site Occupancy Survey (Glacier 2012)

Initial pika site occupancy survey (Glacier 2012)

Park: GLAC	Site ID:	Observer/s:	Circle name of observer who conducted search	Date:

Trail name:			Distance of site from trail:	Azimuth of site from trail:

Spot to leave trail	GPS acc. (m):	UTM Zone:	Easting:	Northing:	Points	Averaged? YES NO
Site center	GPS acc. (m):	UTM Zone:	Easting:	Northing:	Points	Averaged? YES NO

Arrival time:	Begin time for scat/hay search:		End time for scat/hay search:	Departure time:

Pika sign (types = Pika Sighting, **Pika Call**, **Fresh Haypile**, **Old Haypile**, **Fresh Scat**, **Old Scat**)

	Time (24-hr)	Sign type (PS, PC, FH, OH, FS, OS)	Distance (m) from site center	If FS, approx. # of pellets If OS, approx. # of pellets Categories: <5, 5-9, 10-50, 51-100, >100	Notes
1					
2					
3					
4					
5					
6					
7					
8					
9					
10					

Initial pika site occupancy survey (Glacier 2012)

Vegetation cover (% class*) in site	Rock:	Bare:	Grass:	Forb:	Shrub:	Tree:

*Percent classes: 0, T (<1%), 1-5, 5-25, 25-50, 50-76, 75-95, 95-100, 100

Site Notes (include description of area to turn on GPS unit, any hazards encountered, and distance of site from talus edge [if applicable]):

Plot Observation Notes (specific to that day's survey and could include other wildlife observations, etc.):

Photos: (coordinates only necessary if taken outside the site. Also, if need space for additional photos, use the notes section or the edge of the data form.)

1. Camera: _____ Initial name: _____ Azimuth to center (°): _____
   Dist. to center (m): _____
   Description: _____ Final name: _____ .jpg

2. Camera: _____ Initial name: _____ Azimuth to center (°): _____
   Dist. to center (m): _____
   Description: _____ Final name: _____ .jpg

3. Camera: _____ Initial name: _____ Azimuth to center (°): _____
   Dist. to center (m): _____
   Description: _____ Final name: _____ .jpg

4. Camera: _____ Initial name: _____ Azimuth to center (°): _____
   Dist. to center (m): _____
   Description: _____ Final name: _____ .jpg

5. Camera: _____ Initial name: _____ Azimuth to center (°): _____
   Dist. to center (m): _____
   Description: _____ Final name: _____ .jpg

Site diagram:

Sketch sign locations (w/# from opposite page) and other useful information (e.g. landmarks, marker location, etc.)

N

W   E

Appendix C. Data Form 3 –High Country Citizen Science Pika Survey Form (Glacier 2012)

GLACIER NATIONAL PARK HIGH COUNTRY CITIZEN SCIENCE PIKA SURVEY FORM (2012)

| Date: | Observer (s): (circle person who conducted search) | | Phone/Email: | |

Citizen Science Hours (includes driving, hiking & survey time)

| | | Time at start of day: | Time at end of day: |

| Trail Name: | | Number of miles hiked: | Site Name (#): (on marker and/or map) |

| Arrival time at site: | Begin time for traverse search: | End time for traverse search: | Departure time from site: |

TIME AND TYPE OF PIKA DETECTION (*Please write "none" if no pikas or sign observed during survey.*)
PIKA DETECTION TYPES = Pika Sighting, Pika Call, Fresh Haypile, Old Haypile, Fresh Scat, Old Scat
*For the number of pellets, approximate into the following categories: <5, 5-10, 11-50, 51-100, >100

	Time of detection	Detection type (may list multiples per location)	Distance (m) from site center	If fresh scat. # of pellets*	If old scat, # of pellets*	Verification photo (Y/N)	Comments (Other wildlife and/or sign, uncertain detections, etc.)
1							
2							
3							
4							
5							
6							
7							
8							
9							
10							

| Estimate % cover for each ground cover type (0, <1, 1-5, 5-25, 25-50, 50-75, 75-95, 95-100, or 100%): | Rock: | Bare ground (dirt, mineral soil, plant debris/ sticks): | Grass: | Forb (non-woody plants): | Shrub: | Tree: |

CONTINUE ON REVERSE

20

GLACIER NATIONAL PARK HIGH COUNTRY CITIZEN SCIENCE PIKA SURVEY FORM (2012)

Please rate the following for this site on a scale of 1-5 (1 very easy; 5 very difficult):

Ability to reach the talus field	1	2	3	4	5	NA
Ability to traverse talus	1	2	3	4	5	NA
Ability to navigate to/locate the site marker	1	2	3	4	5	NA
Ability to follow/understand the instructions and survey methods	1	2	3	4	5	NA
Ability to identify pikas	1	2	3	4	5	NA
Ability to identify pika sign	1	2	3	4	5	NA
Ability to age pika haypiles and scat	1	2	3	4	5	NA
Ability to complete search in allotted time	1	2	3	4	5	NA
Ability to estimate vegetation cover	1	2	3	4	5	NA

Approx. time to locate marker from trail (minutes):

Why did you select this site (check all that apply):
____ Scenic location ____ Safety consideration
____ New area of park
____ Optimal hiking distance/strenuousness
____ Optimal driving time/convenience
____ Other: _____

If last survey of the day, how many sites did you survey today: ____ sites

Notes, comments, or general feedback:

Surveys should not be conducted in inclement weather such as rain, snow, high winds

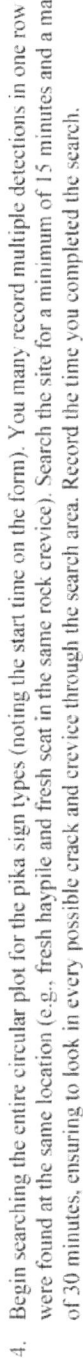

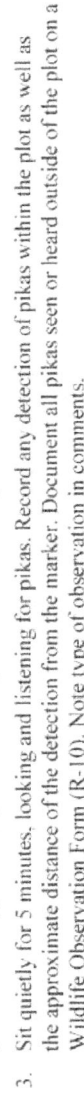

PIKA SURVEY PROCEDURES

Survey equipment: Measuring tape/cord, pin flags, and GPS unit.
Recommended: Leather gloves, camera, flashlight, and watch.

1. Navigate to survey site using route map. GPS point location and photo of reference on trail. Once close (~10 m) begin looking for the metal site marker and/or rock cairn. Once you find the site marker*, enter the site number as "Site Name" on the data form. *If you cannot find the site marker after some time (>30 minutes), move on to another site and notify the citizen science coordinator.

2. Use the measuring tape or cord to measure out 12-m to four edges of the plot, leaving a pin flag at each edge (see right). This will help you establish/visualize the search area. Note. Sometimes the plot will extend beyond the talus but you should still use same site center and plot edges. In these cases, all rock in the plot should be searched and all ground cover types in the plot, even if beyond the talus, incorporated in the cover estimates.

3. Sit quietly for 5 minutes, looking and listening for pikas. Record any detection of pikas within the plot as well as the approximate distance of the detection from the marker. Document all pikas seen or heard outside of the plot on a Wildlife Observation Form (R-10). Note type of observation in comments.

4. Begin searching the entire circular plot for the pika sign types (noting the start time on the form). You many record multiple detections in one row if those were found at the same location (e.g., fresh haypile and fresh scat in the same rock crevice). Search the site for a minimum of 15 minutes and a maximum of 30 minutes, ensuring to look in every possible crack and crevice through the search area. Record the time you completed the search.

5. Estimate the percent cover for each ground cover type and complete survey questionnaire (above).

6. Return survey forms ASAP by fax (406) 888-7903, or email glac_citizen_science@nps.gov, or mail GNP-CCRLC, PO Box 128, West Glacier, MT 59936

OTHER PIKAS SEEN DURING HIKE (OUTSIDE OF SURVEY PERIODS OR SURVEY PLOT):

Time at detection	Detection type (may list multiple types per location)	UTM's (NAD 83) Easting	UTM's (NAD 83) Northing	Specific location (mountain, aspect, trail mileage, etc.)	Comments

NPS 117/119606, January 2013